The Chinese Struggle to Struggle to America:

An Immigration History

by Gail K. Gordon

Scott Foresman
is an imprint of

Glenview, Illinois • Boston, Massachusetts • Chandler, Arizona
Upper Saddle River, New Jersey

A Nation of Immigrants

Sometimes people describe the United States as a "nation of immigrants." Since the vast majority of this country's population either moved here from another country or descended from ancestors who immigrated sometime within the last 500 years, those facts alone seem to make it true that the United States is indeed a nation of immigrants.

People from the British Isles, Europe, South America, Africa, Asia, and from every part of the world have come to the United States, seeking adventure, opportunity, and relief from **oppression** and poverty. Tragically, some did not come of their own free will.

In the pages that follow, we will look at the history of the immigration of Chinese people to the United States and what motivated them to leave China. We will ask what they found when they arrived and how they survived. Finally, we will begin to see how the United States changed them, and how they changed the United States.

Why They Came

Over the centuries, the Chinese have not regarded themselves as people who leave their homeland with the intention of permanently settling in another country. Traditionally, they leave only when conditions force them to leave; even then, they hope to return to the land of their ancestors. Nevertheless, in the nineteenth century, Chinese immigrants came to the United States in great numbers. Why did they leave the land of their birth, their villages, and their families?

Conditions in nineteenth-century China were difficult. A drought had caused famine. Merchants and farmers were failing, and craftspeople were losing their clients to industrialization.

As the economy weakened, a **corrupt** government imposed higher taxes on the hungry population. In 1850, the Taiping Rebellion broke out. For more than a decade, people suffered from hunger and fear, and millions died.

In contrast, on the west coast of the United States, people were finding gold in the hills and rivers. In 1848, James W. Marshall, a carpenter who was working in John Sutter's Mill near Coloma, California, discovered gold. Marshall formed a partnership with Sutter, and the men agreed to keep quiet about the gold, but such a secret could not be kept for long. Word of the possibility of enormous wealth spread. In the following year, 80,000 fortune seekers, called the "forty-niners," arrived in California to seek their fortunes in the gold fields.

Prospectors who flocked to California to find their fortunes in the gold fields lived in temporary camps and quickly built towns.

AN ACCOUNT OF
CALIFORNIA,
AND THE
WONDERFUL GOLD REGIONS.

A New Arrival at the Gold Diggings.

WITH A DESCRIPTION OF

he Different Routes to California;
tion about the Country, and the Ancient and
Modern Discoveries of Gold;
est Precious Metals; Accounts of Gold Hunters;
TOGETHER WITH MUCH OTHER

Reading for those going to Cali-
ia, or having Friends th

5

In the Days of the Gold Rush

In China, California would become known as the Golden Mountain. Families placed their hope on a "sojourner," a man of the family who would travel to California, find gold, and return to China with money to buy land and build a better life for all of them. Unlike other immigrants, these men did not hope to bring their families to the United States; they hoped to return to China—someday.

When the first men from China arrived, the white people of California welcomed them because they needed workers. The men arrived wearing traditional quilted jackets, loose trousers that reached their knees, and enormous round bamboo hats on their heads. At first, their unfamiliar clothes and traditions were "exotic," not threatening.

In 1851, more than 3,000 Chinese sojourners arrived at the California docks. Just one year later, more than 20,000 men left China for the Golden Mountain, most of them planning to mine gold. Soon, one-third of the gold miners in the Golden State were Chinese.

A Chinese mining camp of the California Gold Rush period

Many of these miners from China not only brought skills and knowledge of mining, they also brought their own mining tools. For generations, Chinese men had worked the gold mines of Borneo, where they had become successful, even expert, miners. Those men who did not have personal experience mining would have learned from those who did.

In contrast, most of the white miners began their mining venture knowing little or nothing about mining gold but were just looking to "get rich quick." They had the advantage, because California passed laws saying that only whites could prospect for new claims or register them legally. These inexperienced white miners often took the surface gold and then sold their claims to Chinese or Mexican miners, who had the knowledge, skill, or ambition necessary to dig deeper and find more gold. Mexican miners introduced the **cradle**, and Chinese miners learned how to use it to great advantage. Like a child's cradle, this tool was made from a box mounted on rockers. Dirt was poured into the container, then water. Men rocked the cradle until the ordinary dirt was washed away, leaving the heavier gold in the bottom of the container.

The Chinese were not only experts in their use of the cradle, but they also improved on other methods of mining. While most miners used a mesh-bottomed pan to find gold in the creeks and rivers, the Chinese miners used the Chinese pump, a water wheel with a mechanical system of buckets on a rope pulley. With this new mechanism, which they had adapted from the pumps used in rice paddies back in China, they drained large portions of waterways quickly. The white miners were astonished and quickly felt threatened by the **ingenuity** of these tireless workers.

Envious white miners began to chase Chinese miners from claims. As the white men's initial curiosity and tolerance became replaced by bigotry and hatred, they banded together to threaten, intimidate, and attack Chinese miners to keep them from working their claims.

Soon, California passed a law imposing a tax on "foreign" miners. As the tax steadily increased, Chinese miners were forced to abandon mining or work for white mine operators, which decreased their profits.

After the easy surface mining ceased to produce significant amounts of gold, mine operators needed to sink shafts and blast rock. Chinese workers proved to be knowledgeable and skillful in this kind of mining as well. Once again, jealous white miners were **vengeful**, and they pressured mine operators to fire Chinese workers in favor of white workers.

Chinese miners, however, were motivated to keep working. They needed to send money to their families back home, and they continued to work toward the day when they, too, could return home to build better lives.

As the quest for gold spread to other states in the American west, Chinese miners packed their tools and traveled to Montana, Colorado, Washington, Oregon, and even Canada. Just as they had in the California gold fields, the Chinese miners worked successfully on the claims abandoned by white miners. By 1870, Chinese miners made up one-quarter of all the western miners.

Discrimination by Law

As Chinese workers succeeded where white workers failed, resentment grew. The white men's initial **benign** curiosity at the physical appearance, clothing, and customs of the Chinese turned to cruel ridicule. Newspapers and other periodicals printed offensive caricatures of the Chinese.

The Foreign Miners' Tax law discriminated against these immigrants, while the state of California profited enormously. By 1870, this tax was producing between 25 percent and 50 percent of the state's revenue.

Even the courts were anti-Chinese. In 1854, the California Supreme Court ruled that if a white man was charged with murder, he could not be convicted on the testimony of a Chinese witness. Then in 1882, the U.S. Congress passed the now **infamous** Chinese Exclusion Act, which was unlike any immigration law ever passed before.

This law did not aim to exclude Chinese teachers, merchants, students, or tourists. It aimed to exclude the laborers who worked in mining, on the railroad, or in farming. Because the law proved difficult to enforce, another law was enacted. The Scott Act of 1888 banned the immigration of new Chinese laborers and prevented the return of Chinese laborers who had left the United States to return home temporarily.

Racist cartoons such as this one appeared frequently in the popular press of the time. Such cartoons fueled the growing ill will between the Chinese and the white populations.

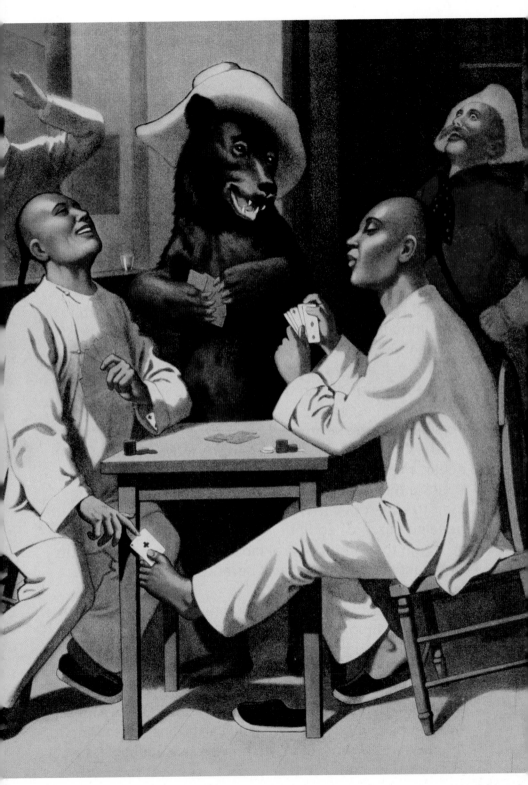

On May 10, 1869, the "golden spike" that linked the Union Pacific Railroad with the Central Pacific Railroad was driven into place. This image commemorates the occasion, but the Chinese workers were not included in the picture.

The Railroad Builders

As the rush to find gold slowed, another race began. In 1861, the Central Pacific Railway was formed to lay track for the transcontinental railroad from Sacramento, California, eastward. The Union Pacific Company was formed to lay track from Omaha, Nebraska, westward. The ultimate goal was to join the two sets of tracks and form a railway that crossed the continent. Everyone saw the value in shrinking the travel time between the older eastern cities and the new western settlements. Businessmen especially saw the enormous profit possibility of this venture.

The Central Pacific, which had the most difficult task, began work in 1863. This company's planned route took the rails through the hard rock of mountains and along their treacherous cliffs. They also had to contend with freezing blizzards and punishing deserts. The men had to be tough to do this physical labor. Young Irish immigrants who had left their homeland because of famine signed on for the work.

In the first two years of work, only fifty miles of track were completed on the Central Pacific line. The challenging conditions defeated many workers, and their bosses found it difficult to replace them with willing and able new recruits. All that changed in 1865 when they decided to hire the Chinese laborers. Soon, 3,000 Chinese men were at work on the Central Pacific line, and hiring agents were eager to sign on more of these reliable, fast, and skilled workers.

Climbing sheer cliff faces to plant explosives was
challenging and added danger to an already **hazardous**
job. Again, the Chinese applied not only their physical
strength but also their intelligence to this job. They
conquered the mountains by engineering a new method
of scaling the steep cliffs. Using reeds, they wove large,
strong baskets to carry men, as a pulley system hauled
them up the rock face. The men then drilled holes in the
rock and planted the dynamite that blasted away the
rock to make way for the railroad. Building the railroad
was dangerous—even deadly—work, and many brave
and determined Chinese men died in its accomplishment.

Chinatown

Most of the Chinese men who first embarked on the clipper ships to California were unmarried. A great many later returned to China temporarily to marry and begin a family before they returned to the United States to continue working for enough money to buy a piece of land in China. A few succeeded financially and realized that dream—although it may have taken a decade or two. Most did not realize their dream of returning to their homeland. They sent money, worked, and hoped.

These workers wanted to form communities where they could follow their own ways and culture. Thus, the vibrant Chinatowns of San Francisco, New York City, and other cities sprang up across the country.

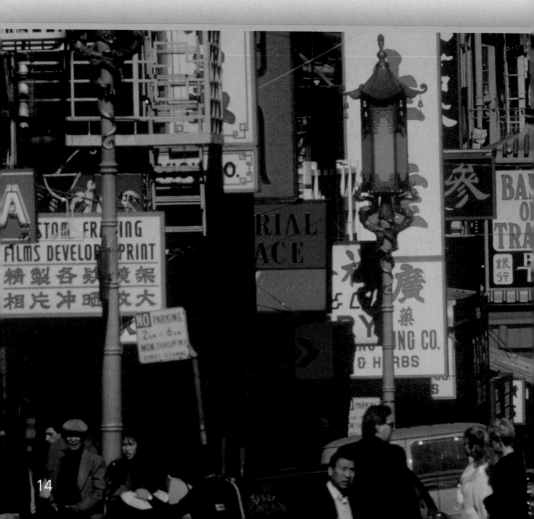

The men were accustomed to forming associations based on the **clan** they came from. These associations helped newcomers find jobs and lodging; they established scholarships and offered loans. The clan always took care of its poor, sick, and elderly. In the 1850s, the Chinese Six Companies was formed and became rather powerful, especially in representing the Chinese community in dealings with government officials.

As more Chinese came to the United States, the Chinatown merchants operated laundries and opened markets. Visitors to the areas were amazed at the exotic and unfamiliar items, including strange foodstuffs, to be found in the markets.

The Food Basket of America

Before California's long growing season could produce rich crops, the swamps had to be drained to produce arable soil. It was the Chinese laborer who contributed to this effort.

When mining in the gold fields decreased, many Chinese laborers were hired by farmers who knew that the soil of the swamps must be rich and fertile. They also knew the reputation the Chinese workers had of being tough, reliable, and skillful.

Chinese workers built miles of ditches and dikes to control the water, and by so doing, they turned previously unused land into productive property. They built roads, bridges, and fences. When the land was ready, the Chinese planted, tended, and harvested the crops. By the 1870s, three-quarters of all farm workers in California were Chinese.

They were not well compensated for their endeavors. As had happened so many times before (and as has happened so many times since), the land owners got rich while the Chinese laborers barely survived on low wages. Racial and cultural prejudice meant that well-paying jobs were not available to them. They were rarely successful in protesting their low wages. In spite of the poor treatment, however, the Chinese workers still applied their knowledge and skills—whether it be in the gold fields, on the railroad, or on farms. In China, they had grown vegetables and fruit, grains and beans, and now they used their wealth of experience to help turn California into the agricultural center it is today.

The white Californians of the nineteenth century were beef eaters, not particularly interested in eating fish. Yet, fish was a mainstay of the Chinese diet, so Chinese fishermen used their traditional designs for boats and the fishing lore they had brought with them from China to harvest the Pacific Coast's fishing-grounds for herring, sturgeon, and even shark. They ran fish camps and salmon canneries. They fed their own people, and eventually, even the white people developed a taste for the fish that the Chinese were bringing ashore.

Construction of the Immigration Station on Angel Island in San Francisco Bay began in 1905. The detention facility began operations in 1910.

Angel Island

Angel Island, located in an area of San Francisco Bay called China Cove, was chosen for its remoteness as a detention station for immigrants. Opened in 1910, it served as the point of entry for most of the Chinese immigrating to the United States for the next thirty years. Approximately 175,000 Chinese people came through Angel Island. Most stayed for two to three weeks, but some stayed much longer, waiting for clearance to enter the country or for deportation.

The Chinese Exclusion Act that had prohibited most Chinese laborers from entering the United States had been renewed in 1892 and again in 1902. Some white Americans were determined to keep the cheap and skilled competition out. At the same time, some Chinese immigrants were desperate to bring others from their villages to work and earn money in the United States. This desperation led to a phenomenon called "paper sons."

"Paper sons" purchased false papers that identified them as sons of Chinese men who had become citizens of the United States, because the son of a citizen was automatically a citizen as well. But a "paper son" had to keep his story consistent with that of the man claiming to be his father. Immigration officials detained all Chinese at Angel Island to determine if their papers were legitimate and their lineage was as they claimed. Many Chinese carved poems into the walls as they waited and suffered on Angel Island; some of these poems can still be seen today, even though the station closed in 1940.

Chinese Americans Today

Finally, in 1943, the Chinese Exclusion Act was repealed. A quota system remained in place, however, allowing only 105 Chinese to enter the country each year. Still, Chinese Americans could now become naturalized citizens. The existing Chinese American community welcomed the arrival of more women from China, including the wives of Chinese American soldiers who married Chinese women during World War II.

Although racism and prejudice were not entirely eliminated, attitudes began to change. In 1959, Hawaii became the fiftieth state in the union, which was an important turning point for Chinese Americans, as most Hawaiians came from Asian ancestry. In fact, Hawaii's first U.S. Senator was a Chinese American.

Yo-Yo Ma, world famous cellist

Maya Yang Lin, architect and designer of the Vietnam War Memorial

In 1989, a group of students in China demonstrated in Tiananmenn Square in Beijing. They wanted freedom and democracy and risked their lives for the same ideals that people in the United States hold. Many Chinese students studying in the United States were afraid to return to China and its repressive government, and so the United States government granted them permission to stay.

Today many Chinese Americans still struggle, as other minorities do, to overcome the effects of decades of discrimination. But it can no longer be denied that Chinese Americans have made and continue to make outstanding contributions to life in the United States.

Amy Tan, author of best-selling novels

Hiram Fong, the first Chinese American to be elected to the U.S. Senate

Now Try This

Building the Railroad: A Worker's Diary

Unfortunately, the Chinese workers who built the railroad left very few written accounts of their experiences. We know that they lived together in camps along the way and that the white people working with them thought the Chinese ways were strange. For instance, they brought with them a supply of warm tea to drink all day. But the white workers thought the strangest practice was that the Chinese workers wore clean clothes and bathed every day! We also know, of course, that they worked very hard. Put yourself in a Chinese worker's place; imagine a series of journal entries that he might have written.

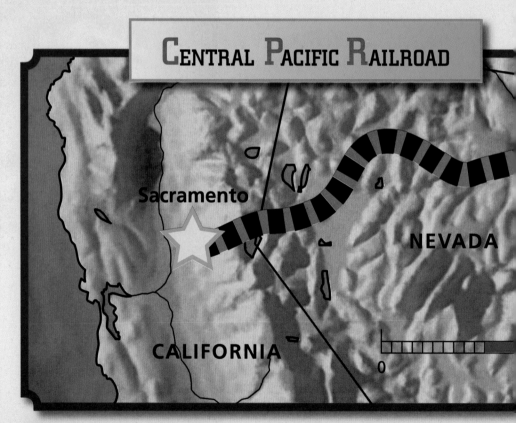

CENTRAL PACIFIC RAILROAD

Sacramento

NEVADA

CALIFORNIA

0

1. Choose three places along the route from the map below. Be sure to choose one place in the mountains, one place in the desert, and one place near a town. You may need to do a little research for this at the library or on the Internet.

2. It is time to make your first journal entry. Be sure to note the date and the place. Describe the weather that day, your surroundings, and the kind of work completed that day.

3. You have moved on to another location. Describe the new area. Imagine the challenging weather that day. Describe the conditions. How did they affect your work?

4. Again you have moved along the line. Describe where you are. Do you miss your family? How do you feel about the fact that white workers are receiving a higher salary than you? Record your feelings in your journal.

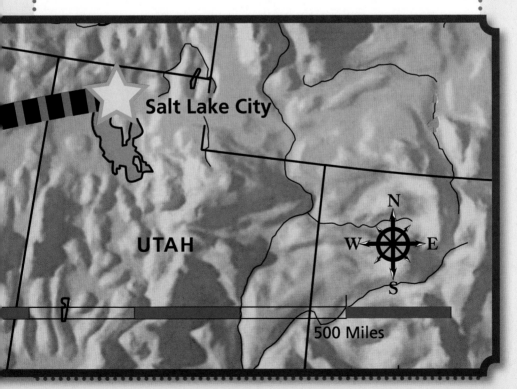

Salt Lake City

UTAH

N
W E
S

500 Miles

Glossary

benign *adj.* kind or gentle; unthreatening

clan *n.* a group of families related through a common ancestor or through marriage

corrupt *adj.* dishonest; swayed by bribery or influence

cradle *n.* a mining device consisting of a frame with rods like fingers to separate materials, mounted on rockers to allow a back-and-forth movement

hazardous *adj.* full of risk; dangerous

infamous *adj.* having a very bad reputation; notorious

ingenuity *n.* skill in planning or making; cleverness

oppression *n.* cruel or unjust treatment

vengeful *adj.* feeling or showing a strong desire for vengeance, or returning a wrong